So there's going to be a **new baby** in your family? And you'll soon be a **big brother** or **big sister?** Here's a special book just for you to help you welcome your new baby.

Other Marlor Press books for Kids:

Kid's Vacation Diary

Kid's Address & Writing Book

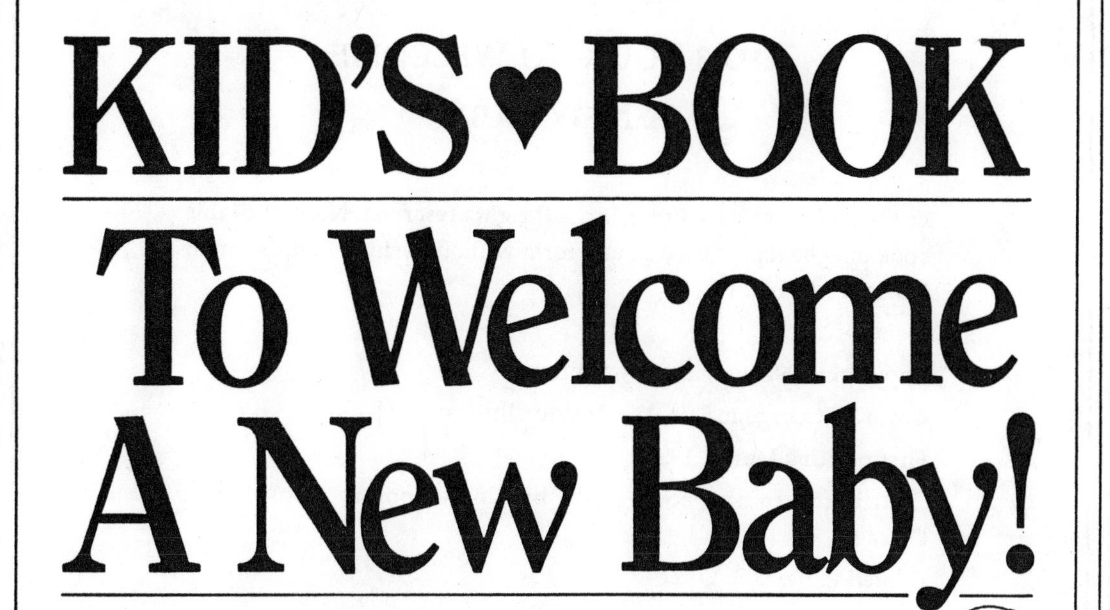

KID'S ♥ BOOK To Welcome A New Baby!

A fun activity book of things to do and to learn for a "big brother" or "big sister"

BARBARA J. COLLMAN

Published by Marlor Press, Inc.

KID'S BOOK TO WELCOME A NEW BABY

Cover by Georgene Sainati   Inside illustrations by Marlin Bree

First printing March, 1992

Distributed to the book trade by Contemporary Books, Inc., Chicago

Printed in the U.S.A.

ISBN 0-943400-65-1

Marlor Press Inc.

4304 Brigadoon Drive \ Saint Paul, MN 55126

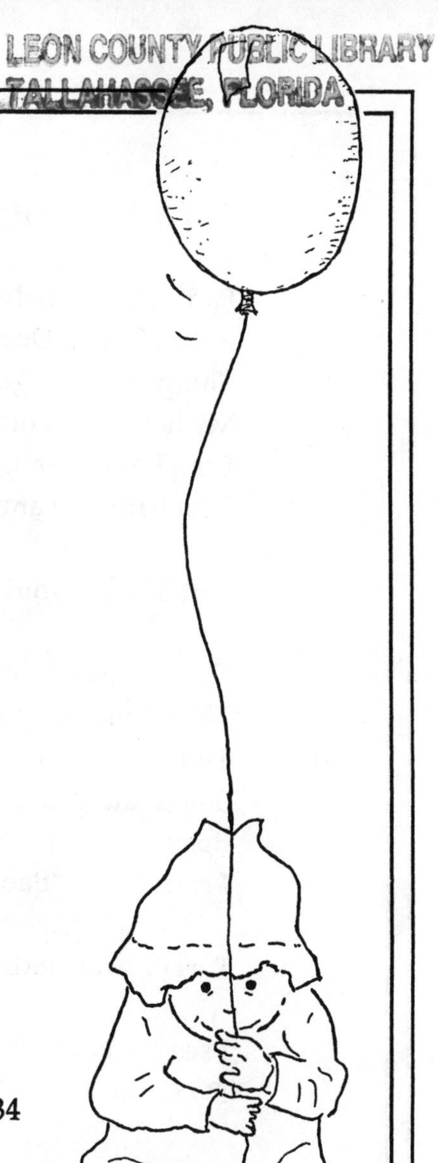

Contents

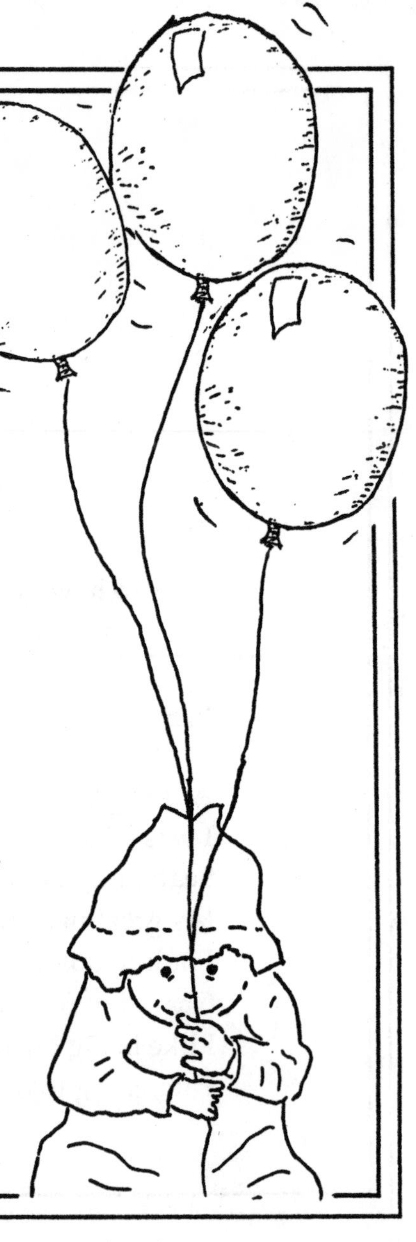

KIDS!

How to have fun with this book!

Something exciting is happening in your family! Your mom and dad have told you that there will be a new baby in your family. You soon will have a baby brother or a baby sister! The *Kid's Book to Welcome a New Baby* will help you get ready to be a *great* big sister or big brother.

You can start today to read and do the activities in this book. You will learn many fun and important things about babies and about how to keep them safe. Your mom and dad will be pleased with all that you will learn. Remember that you will always need permission to play with your new little brother or sister.

Part 1 is called *All about me.* Here you can write fun things about when you were a baby as well as some interesting facts about yourself now. Have you ever looked at two photos of yourself at the same time—one when you were a baby and one of you *now?*

Part 2 is called *My family gets ready.* It is full of ideas for projects to make and do while you are waiting for the new baby. You can even keep track of the ways you help with your own *Helping Record.*

Part 3 is *All about babies.* Here you can learn how your mom and dad will take care of your new brother or sister. You can find out how you can help. You can earn your own *I am Baby-Ready Certificate* .

Part 4 is *Welcoming the new baby.* It will help you get to know your sister or brother right away. You can find out what the new baby can do and you can watch how he or she spends one whole day. You can paste in photographs of you and the baby and learn the best ways to play together.

Part 5 is called *We grow up together.* That's because that is what brothers and sisters do. As you watch your baby sister or baby brother grow and learn, you can write down each important step. You can find out what other brothers and sisters liked about growing up together.

Pretty soon, the new baby at your house will not be so new. Day by day and week by week, there will be more and more things you can do with your new brother or sister. This book will hold many memories of fun times spent together growing up.

A special note to parents

This book will help your child welcome a new baby. It will encourage interest in the baby and in becoming a big sister or brother. The activities are designed to open up family discussions and can be easily adapted to your child's age and abilities. Reading and working together in this book will let your child know that he or she is an important member of the family.

You can use **Part 1,** *All about me* **Part 2,** *My family gets ready,* and **Part 3,** *All about babies,* from the time you choose to tell your child of the expected baby until his or her actual arrival.

Part 1, *All about me,* emphasizes the child's own birth, early childhood, and recent accomplishments.

Part 2, *My family gets ready,* lets your child help with the family's preparations for the new baby and makes both the creative and the routine tasks more fun.

Together you will plan such things as a birth announcement and special parent-child times for after the baby arrives.

Part 3, *All about babies,* introduces your child to baby care and safety. You will set the procedures and practices for your home, and, of course, your older child will always need your supervision when helping with the baby.

This section also prepares the child for the hectic and critical first days after the baby comes home.

As soon as the new baby arrives, your child will go on to **Part 4,** *Welcoming the new baby.* He or she can record the birth statistics, paste in photographs, and creatively discover things about a new baby as well as what the baby likes and can do. There are guidelines for playtime and a chart to record your child's and baby's first activities together.

The last section, **Part 5,** *We grow up together,* encourages your son or daughter to look forward to the days ahead to learn more about what having a new brother or sister really means.

Your child can keep track of baby's firsts and prepare a special message to be kept for later.

Your family can benefit from this book in many ways. You, the parents, will relax as you anticipate a smoother transition for every member of your family. You'll watch your child welcome the new baby with increased acceptance and love.

Your child will have a foundation to become a responsible big brother or big sister. He or she will have received extra attention and support from you and will be ready to participate in this important family event.

Before and after the baby arrives, your child will have educational and entertaining activities to keep busy. He or she will be challenged to be a *great* big brother or big sister.

The new baby will come into a family which is better prepared for the adjustment period. He or she will find a sibling more ready to care. *Kid's Book to Welcome a New Baby* will prepare your home to welcome the new member of the family.

PART 1

ALL ABOUT ME!

A special baby you know ✩

Your mom and dad waited for a special baby to be born. That baby was **YOU!**

Activity: What is a family?

Use pictures cut from catalogs and magazines to make a poster. On one side, put pictures of things that might be in any **house**--like chairs, beds, or lamps. On the other side, put pictures that show how a family turns a **house** into a **home**, like a mom cooking supper, a dad tucking a child into bed, or a grandma rocking a baby.

I was a baby, too!

My mom and dad were very happy when I became part of the family.

They named me:________________________________

Something special about my name is:__________________

____

Sometimes they called me
by my nickname:________________________________

I WAS BORN ON:

Month________________Day_________Year__________

I was the: _____first child_____second child
_____third child or _________________________child.

Right after I was born, I had: _____*some* hair _____a *little* hair_____*no* hair at all (poor me).

The first day home, I met:

....

....

My favorite song was....

....

...especially if this person sang it to me:

....

A toy I liked to sleep with was:

....

My folks showed me off when they took me here:

....

This is a story about something I did:

....

....

....

....

....

Searching for clues about me!

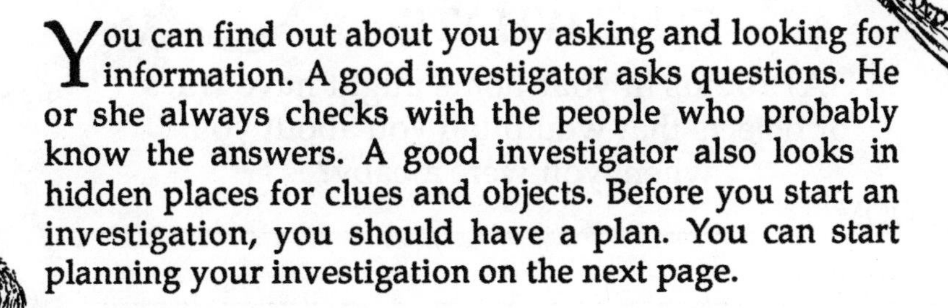

You can find out about you by asking and looking for information. A good investigator asks questions. He or she always checks with the people who probably know the answers. A good investigator also looks in hidden places for clues and objects. Before you start an investigation, you should have a plan. You can start planning your investigation on the next page.

START WITH A PLAN: THE **WHO**

WHO are the people who knew you when you were a baby? Write their names below. They are the best people to answer your questions and help you find clues:

NAME ....

NAME ....

NAME

NAME

NAME

STEP TWO: THE **WHATS**

me

WHAT **rooms** in your home might have clues or objects that would tell you about you when you were a baby?

ROOM

ROOM

ROOM

ROOM

WHAT **places** might have objects that tell about you—but might be hidden away?

PLACE 1

PLACE 2

PLACE 3

PLACE 4

WHAT **documents or things** about you do you think you might find?

....

____

....

....

WHEN do you plan to carry out your investigation?

DATE & TIME ____

DATE & TIME ....

DATE & TIME ....

DATE & TIME ....

DATE & TIME ____

DATE & TIME ....

about me

My great investigation

An investigator must usually write a report telling about the investigation. When you have finished your investigation, write your report here and on the next page:

The date (or dates) of your investigation:

Your assistants in the case:

ME?

Where you conducted (locations) your investigation:

1. ______________________________

2. ______________________________

3. ______________________________

4. ______________________________

What I found as a result of my investigation:

____

____

____

____

____

____

____

____

____

____

____

My conclusions:

I **learned lots** about when I was a baby ____yes_____no.

_____I want to **learn even more** about when I was a baby. Some things I want to know more about are:

1. ....
2. ....
3. ....
4. ....
5. ....

_____My search was **incomplete**. I was not able to find out all I needed to know.

1. ....
2. ....
3. ....
4. ....
5. ....

Finding out about me!

You were able to locate some items which told you a little bit about yourself when you were a baby. Check below those you found:

_____your Birth Certificate_____baby pictures
_____your favorite toys _____some favorite clothes

____And did you hear your birth day story?

Did you find your Birth Certificate?

Here is some information you can find on it:

Length of my footprint: ___________inches
My height:__________inches
My weight:_____ pounds______ounces
Time of my birth:__________a.m. or p.m.?
My doctor's name:_____________________________
My hospital's name__________________________

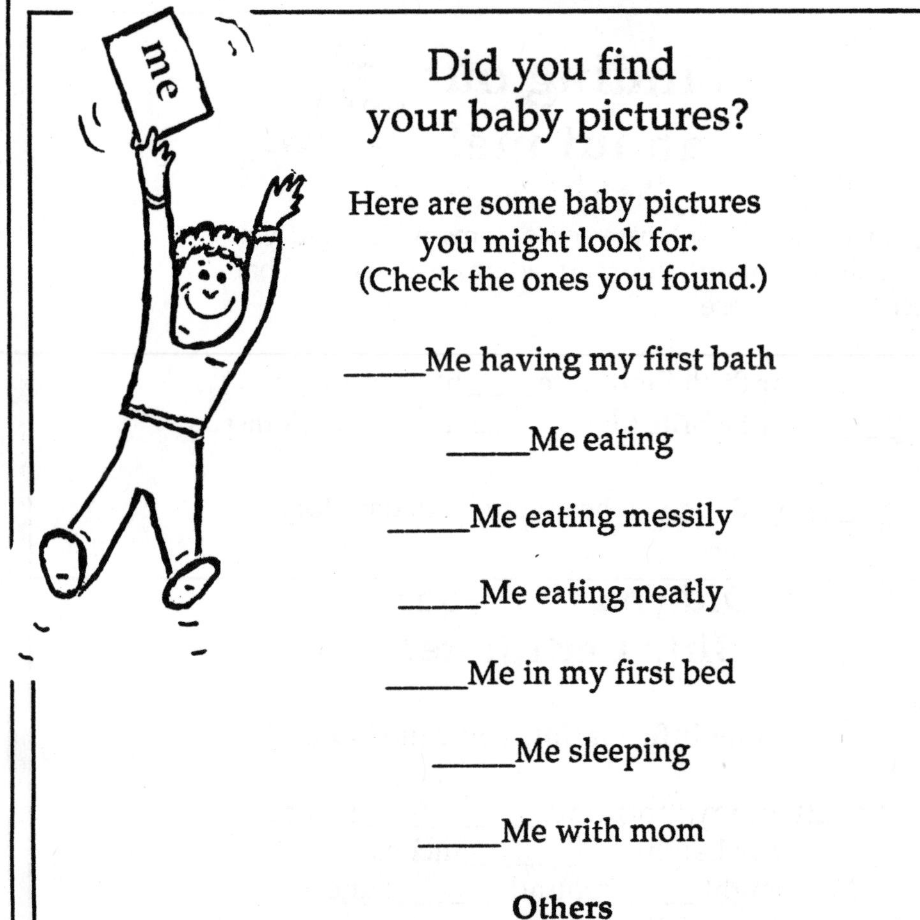

Did you find your baby pictures?

Here are some baby pictures
you might look for.
(Check the ones you found.)

_____Me having my first bath

_____Me eating

_____Me eating messily

_____Me eating neatly

_____Me in my first bed

_____Me sleeping

_____Me with mom

Others

1. ....

2. ....

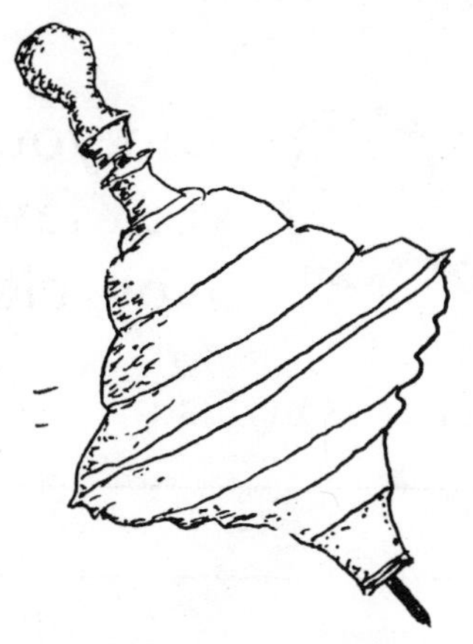

Did you find
your favorite
baby toys?

Here is my list:

1. ....

2. ....

3. ....

4. ....

5. ....

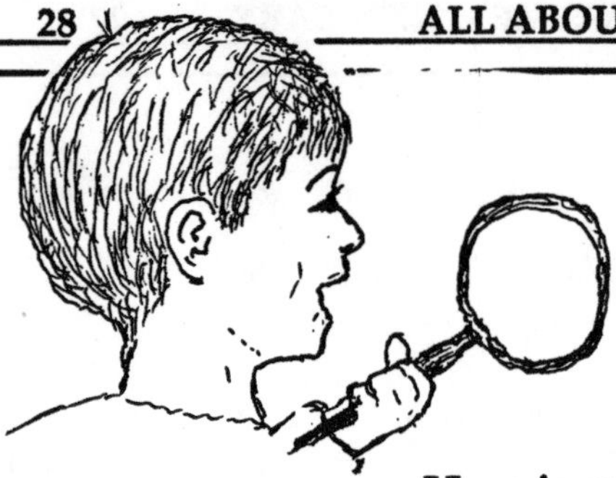

Did you find your favorite baby clothes?

Here is my list:

1. ____________________

2. ____________________

3. ____________________

4. ____________________

Did you hear your birth day story?

Mom and Dad told me the story of my birth day on this date: Month__________day_____year_____

Their Story: ____________________

____

____

____

me

Here's something else interesting about the day I was born:

Changing from baby to big kid!

Here's a picture taken of me
when I was a very, very new baby:

(Paste
your
picture
here)

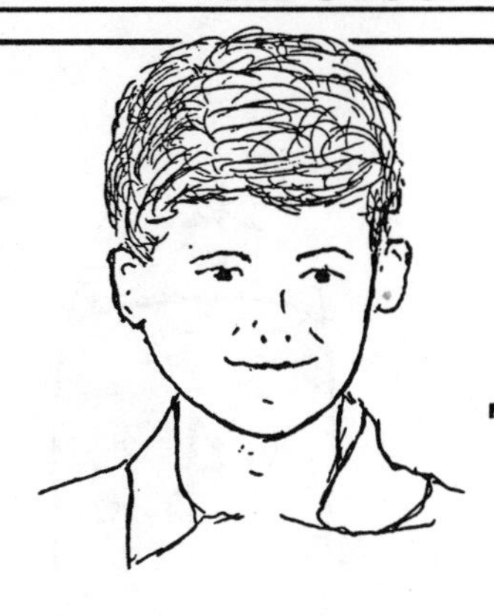

Here's a picture of me TODAY!

(paste your picture here)

I like being BIGGER!

I'm blasting off
to being a big kid!
Here's a countdown
of my experiences

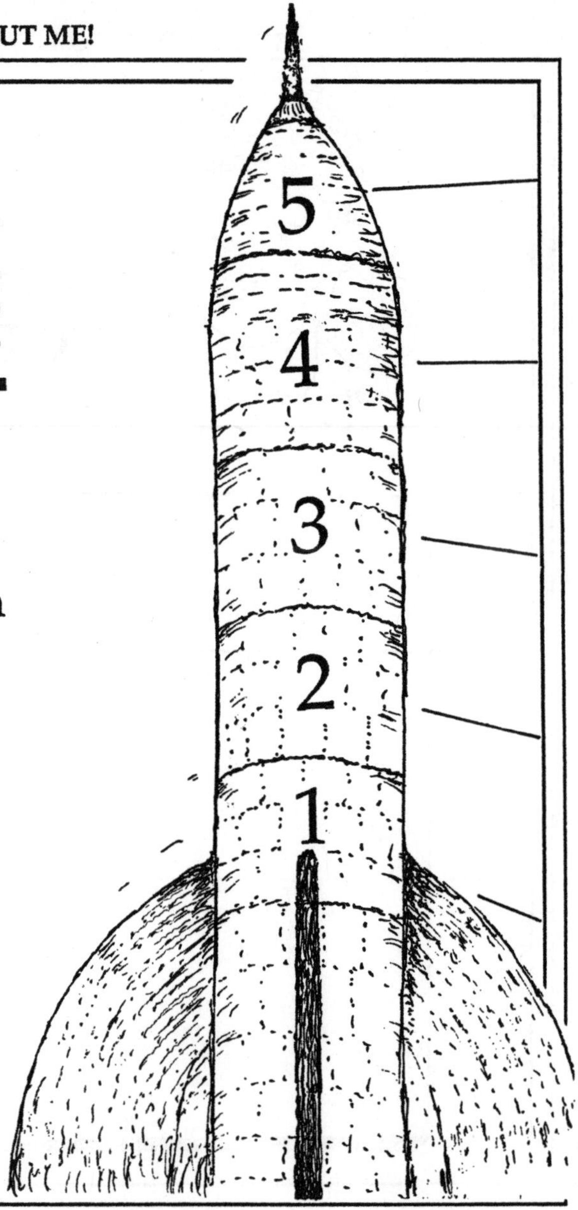

5

4

3

2

1

5 "Big kid" things I have learned to do:
(Tie my shoes? Ride a bike? Get dressed? Other?)

....

....

4 Special places I have visited:
(A zoo?' Circus? Play group?)

....

....

3 Special things I am allowed to do:
(Take lessons? Sleep over?)

....

____

2 Special changes I would like when I become a big brother or big sister:
(More allowance? Bigger bed?)

....

____

1 Special privileges I am hoping for in the future:
(Later bedtime? A pet?)

....

I am going to be a big brother or sister!

You are already a son or daughter, a grandson or granddaughter, and maybe a little brother or sister. Now you will be a **big brother** or **big sister.** Here's a place for you to write how you feel about having a new sister or brother, what you think it will be like, and what you think will be the best part of being the big brother or sister.

PART 2

MY FAMILY GETS READY!

Your family is waiting for
a special baby again!
You are happy and excited—
and busy getting ready!

How many noses?

How many people are NOW
in your family?______

How many girls?______ How many boys?________
How many noses?______ How many ears?________
How many fingers?_____ How many hearts?________

AFTER the baby comes:

How many boys?_______ How many girls?_______
How many noses?_______ How many ears?_______
How many fingers?_____
How many loving hearts?_____

**How many people are in
your family now?_____**

I AM READY TO HELP!

Your mom is busy doing a **very important** job. She is taking care of the **baby** growing inside her. She is working so hard at her special job that she may need extra rest and she may also need extra help.

BRILLIANT BRAIN: *Good to plan a surprise for mom.*

Fill a box, bag or basket with **14 small gifts** (some for her, some for baby.) Tell her to open one every day starting about **two weeks** before the baby might come. For the baby, you can plan a surprise of a small stuffed toy, bib or booties. Additional ideas: You can give mom IOU's for washing dishes or watering the garden, or something else you can think of to help.

EAGLE EYES: *To see when mom needs help. (Like tying her shoelaces.)*

ESCALATOR VOICE: *To go up loud for playing outside and to go down low when mom is resting.*

GRIPPER HANDS: *To carry a pillow for mom's back, slippers for her feet, and a glass of milk.*

RACING FEET: *To run and get whatever mom needs.*

HELPING WITH DUMP DAY!

Your family may be planning a DUMP DAY! That's a day to get out boxes of baby clothes, blankets, bottles and other things the baby will need. On Dump Day, you can help your mom and dad find your old baby things and help get them ready for the new baby.

FIND

the **first toys** the baby will play with, such as:_____ rattles_____soft stuffed animals_____things that can be squeaked____things that are made to be chewed

HELP

wash them and put them in a special box or basket. (Maybe you can decorate it.)

FIND

the **clothes** the baby will wear right away: _____pajamas with feet _____undershirts _____little socks

HELP

wash them and put them away in the baby's own drawers.

FIND OUT

what **other things** your family must get ready: _____putting up the crib _____getting out a car seat_____cleaning a baby bathtub _____buying diapers

THINGS TO DO TO GET READY

HELP your mom and dad by making a list here:

1/ ....

2/ ....

3/ ....

4/ ....

5/ ....

6/ ....

MY HELPING RECORD

Here is a record of some ways I helped our family:

Date **I helped by doing this:**

....

....

....

____

....

....

....

I can hardly wait!

Five handy things to do while you wait:

1. Stitch, color or paint a picture for the baby's room. (Check an art store for coloring posters.) Before you frame it, sign your name and the date. Hang your gift in the baby's room.

2. Make a sign that says, SHHHHHH—BABY IS SLEEPING. Use cardboard or posterboard and decorate the sign. Put the sign in a place you will be certain to see it when you come in from outside. Turn it over until you need it.

3. Decorate a box or bag to hold some special "Mom and me" and "Dad and me" plans. Cut some slips of paper and write one activity you plan to do on each one. You might want, "Bake cookies with mom," or "Take a walk with dad." Put all the slips in the box or bag and mark the outside with the instructions to please draw one or two slips every week.

4. If you like to sew, you might be able to make a toy for the baby. You can get some ideas from books at your public library.

5. Make a special sign to put up on the day the baby comes home. You could draw a picture of your family on the sign and write, "Welcome to our Family."

After you know the baby's name, you could add:

We love you,________________________________

(write the baby's name).

I AM HAPPY TO ANNOUNCE!

Baby birth announcements are a way to tell friends about the new baby. If your mom and dad plan to send announcements, you can use your LICK to STICK the stamps on, and your MIGHT to WRITE the names and addresses.

You can celebrate a new baby, too—by giving specially made announcements to your friends at school or to your neighbors. You can think up your own ideas or choose from one of these in the book. You can start making them while you are waiting for the baby to arrive.

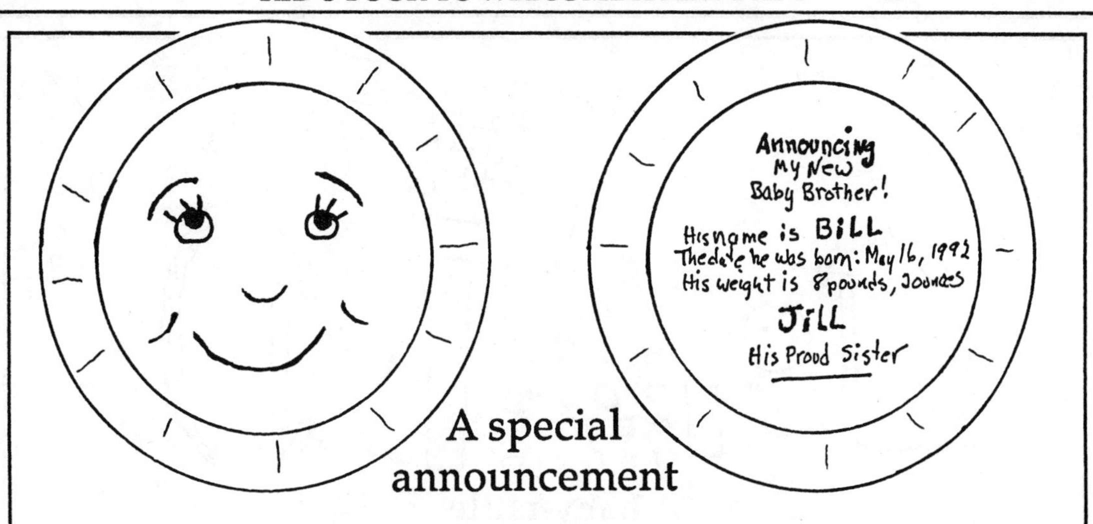

A special announcement

1/ Use a paper plate. 2/ Draw a face with a marker.

3/ Add hair color and eye color to match baby's.

4/ Add a pink hairbow on the top for a girl. Add blue bow tie on the bottom for a boy. 5/ Write the announcement on the other side:

Announcing
my new
baby brother! (or baby sister!)

His or her name__________________________

The date he or she was born_______________

His or her weight________________________

Signed (your name),

His Proud Sister (or Brother)

6/ Give your special announcement to your friends.

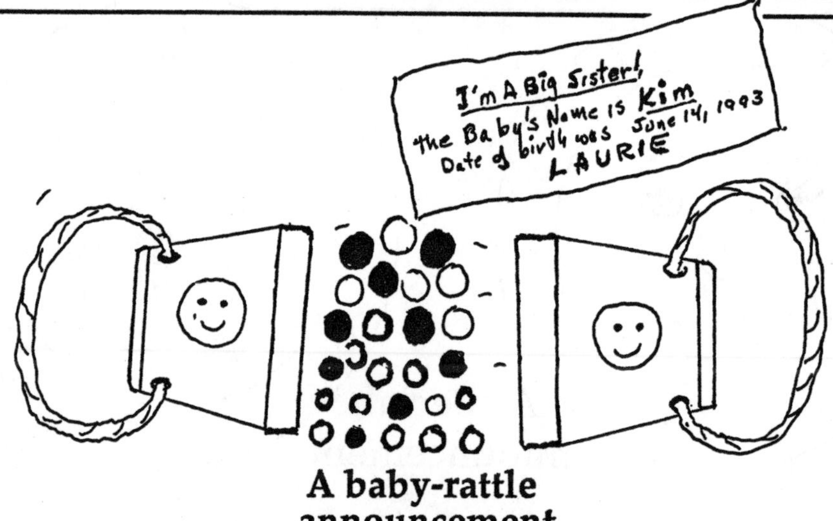

A baby-rattle announcement with a treat!

1/ Use two paper nut cups. 2/ Poke two holes in each cup. 3/ Thread a piece of curling ribbon through the holes. Tie the ribbon on the inside of the cups. 4/ Fill one cup with small candies. 5/ Write an announcement. Roll it up and put it inside.

I'm a Big Sister (Or a Big Brother)
The baby's name____________________
Date of birth________________
Signed, (your name), Big Brother (Or Big Sister)

6/ Glue the rims of the two cups together. 7/Treat your friends to a baby rattle announcement.

PART 3

ALL ABOUT BABIES

You will be a fun big sister
or big brother.
You will want to find out
the most important things
about babies!

The Zoo won't do!

Have you ever seen a baby animal with its mother? It's fun to watch how the mother cares for her baby. But the best way to learn about taking care of a baby brother or sister is to watch a human mother with her family. The pictures here will show you some animal mothers and babies. You can visit a human mother and baby or ask your mom and dad to help you learn about baby care. Then write what you found out!

A mother kangaroo

holds her baby like this:

THE ZOO WON'T DO. I learned to hold a baby like this:

....

....

....

....

A mother cat carries her baby like this:

THE ZOO WON'T DO! I learned to carry a baby this way:

....

....

....

....

A baby panda bear eats this way:

THE ZOO WON'T DO. I learned that a baby eats this way:

....

....

....

____

....

A baby opossum
sleeps like this:

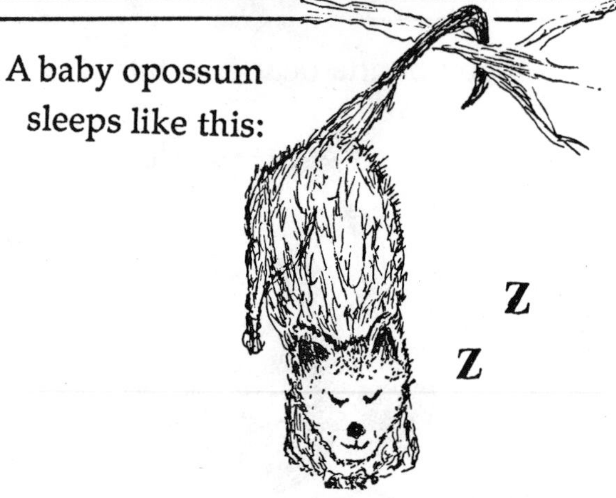

THE ZOO WON'T DO. I learned that a baby sleeps like this:

____

....

....

....

DOLL PRACTICE: Ask your mom or dad to help you practice baby care with a baby doll. You can learn lifting, carrying, holding, burping, feeding, playing, sleeping positions, dressing, washing, and lots more.

Things that I can be!

FOR MOM & DAD, I CAN BE:

___A mail collector
___A diaper fetcher
___A baby checker-upper
___A toy picker-upper
___A message taker
___A list maker
___A laundry folder
___A bottle holder

More ideas (from Mom and Dad):

1. ______________________________
2. ______________________________
3. ______________________________
4. ______________________________
5. ______________________________
6. ______________________________
7. ______________________________
8. ______________________________
9. ______________________________
10. ______________________________

FOR BABY, I CAN BE:

___A music box winder
___A mobile starter
___A baby swing swinger
___A pacifier bringer
___A shoe taker-off-er
___A sit-beside-er
___A player with fingers
___A fantastic singer

More ideas (from Mom and Dad):

....

....

....

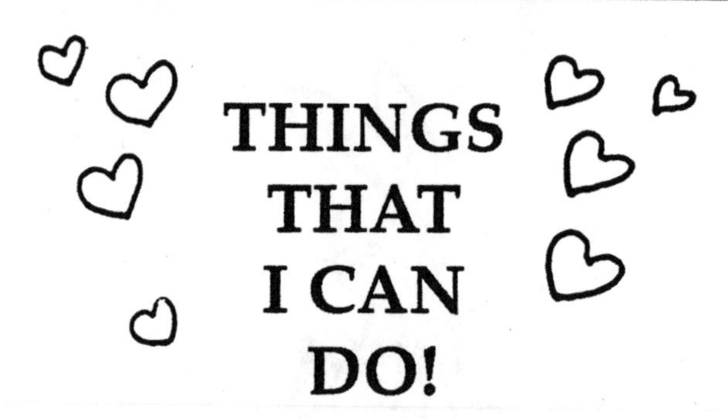

THINGS THAT I CAN DO!

Mom and Dad need me to follow a few rules. We looked at this list below and then we decided I can:

___Pick up the baby when Mom or Dad say it's OK, if I do it the way they tell me to do it.

___Touch the baby very gently with one finger.

___Give the baby food or drinks made just for babies (not mine).

___Give the baby his or her own special toys (not mine).

I realize I am strong, so I must be careful with the baby.

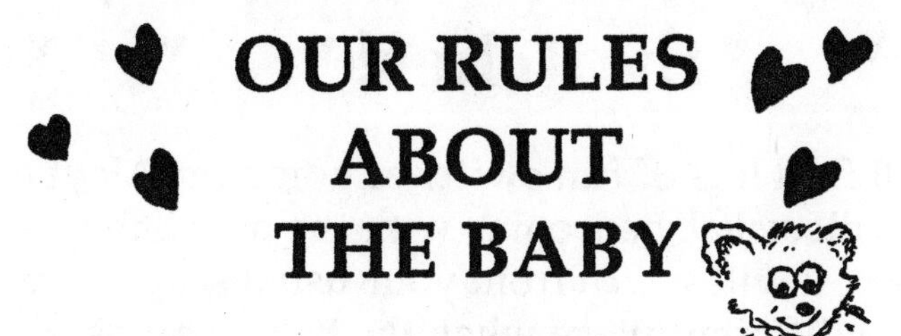

OUR RULES ABOUT THE BABY

1. ....

2. ....

3. ....

4. ....

5. ....

6. ....

7. ....

8. ....

Switches!

You will find lots of fun **switches** going on. Maybe you will *switch* bedrooms with the new baby. Maybe you will *switch* from your usual seat in the car to a different place when the baby's car seat goes in. When baby starts to sit in a high chair, maybe you will *switch* places at the table.

Here is a place to keep track of those *switches* you see, both before and after the new baby comes:

Date: *Switch!* **Why I like the switch:**

1. ______________________________

2. ______________________________

3. ______________________________

4. ______________________________

5. ______________________________

6. ______________________________

7. ______________ ______________

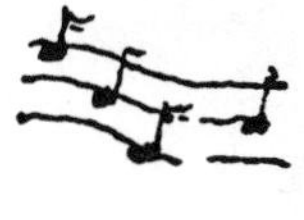

Songs and games to share

Babies love it when you sing to them and play little games with them. Ask your Mom, Dad, and grandparents to teach you their favorite songs and games for babies. You can also ask friends and neighbors, look in books and listen to music.

Name of song I learned: ....

I learned it from: ....

Words of the song: ....

....

....

....

....

....

....

Name of song I learned:

I learned it from:

Words of the song:

Name of song I learned:

I learned it from:

Words of the song:

Name of song I learned: ....

I learned it from: ....

Words of the song: ....

Names
of other songs
I want to remember:

1. ....

2. ....

3. ....

4. ....

5. ....

6. ....

7. ....

8. ....

9. ....

10. ....

FUN GAMES!

Here are some of the games I learned to play with the baby:

Name of game I learned: ______________________

I learned it from: ....

How to play the game: ....

....

____

....

....

....

Name of game I learned:

I learned it from:

How to play the game:

Name of game I learned:

I learned it from:

How to play the game:

Name of game I learned:

I learned it from:

How to play the game:

Name of game I learned:

I learned it from:

How to play the game:

BUSY DAYS!

You are ready for the baby to come and are excited about enjoying your new sister or brother. Here are a few more things you should know about the busy days after the baby comes:

Mom & Dad Busy-ness

____Your Mom will need extra rest. She is tired from her job of caring for the baby—she might have been awake, taking care of the baby while you were asleep.

____Your Dad may be able to stay home from work for a day or two after the baby arrives. He will want to help with the baby, but he will probably have some extra time to play with you, too!

Baby Busy-ness

____The baby may need to go to the doctor's office or hospital for tests or check-ups. There are some special tests that every baby needs, and your parents want to be sure that the baby is healthy.

____The baby will sleep and eat, then sleep and eat, and then sleep and eat again. That's because sleeping and eating are just about all that newborn babies do.

____The baby will cry in between eating and sleeping. You might think at first that something is wrong or that your mom and dad are not trying hard enough, but the baby is probably only crying about as much as any other baby cries. And there are reasons for all that crying!

Family & friends Busy-ness

____People will come to visit. Your family and friends are just as excited about the new baby as you are! Some will come for a short visit; some may stay longer.

____People will call to talk—especially family members who do not live nearby.

Your Busy-ness

You will start doing all the things you have learned—helping your family and helping with the baby.

You will have to pose for lots and lots of pictures!

You will think of things to do with all those pictures:

- Send some pictures to relatives who live far away.

- Make a scrapbook that will be just for pictures of you with your brother or sister. Ask your mom or dad to take a picture every three months; then glue it in your book.

- Make a frame with paper or craft materials. Put a picture of yourself in the frame and place it in the baby's room.

Other Busy-ness for me

(Make a list as you and your parents think of them)

1. ....

2. ....

3. ....

4. ____

5. ....

6. ....

7. ....

I earned my Baby-Ready Certificate

I am Baby-Ready

♥ I practiced baby care.

♥ I helped my family get ready.

♥ I learned songs and games for babies.

♥ I promise to love and protect the new baby in our family.

____

(Signature)

Date________________________

♥

PART 4:

WELCOMING THE NEW BABY!

You have
a new
baby sister
or baby brother!
You will want to get to know
the new baby
right away.

ISN'T THAT A CUTE BABY?

Everybody *loves* babies! If you will listen carefully, you will hear family and friends say many of the same things over and over when they see the new baby. Have you heard someone say these things?

"What an adorable baby!" "The baby looks just like...."
"How tiny!" "You must be so proud!"

Your project is a fun one: **keep a list** of the **things** people say about your new baby. Write down some of these things below. Then, when he or she is older, you can show them to your new brother or sister.

1. ....

2. ....

3. ....

4. ....

5. ....

I see the new baby!

And here is my important record:

Our family's new baby was born on:

____
Day of the week

____
Month Day Year

The baby's full name is:

____
First Name

____
Middle Name

____
Last Name

♥

The baby weighs:

__________ __________
Pounds Ounces

That is (_____more) or (_____less) than
I weighed when I was born.

I weighed:

____
Pounds Ounces

The baby's eyes are this color:______________

I first heard the news of baby's birth from
this person:________________________________

When the baby came, I was at this
location:________________________________

I was busy doing this:__________________________

I first saw the baby on this date:________________

At this location:________________________________

I first held the baby on this date:________________

At this location:

____

My feelings:

....

....

....

♥ ♥ ♥ ♥ ♥ ♥ ♥ ♥ ♥ ♥ ♥
♥ ♥ ♥ ♥ ♥ ♥ ♥ ♥ ♥ ♥ ♥

Now that the baby has arrived...

You can put up the
Welcome Home sign
you made

You can finish and send, or deliver,
the announcements
you made.

♥ ♥ ♥ ♥ ♥ ♥ ♥ ♥ ♥ ♥ ♥
♥ ♥ ♥ ♥ ♥ ♥ ♥ ♥ ♥ ♥ ♥

Do we look alike?

Here is one of the first pictures taken of the baby:

I think baby looks like me
because we have the same:

_____kind of nose _____color of eyes
_____kind of hair _____beautiful smile!

Together:

Here is a picture of

(Baby's name)__________________

and me on this date:_______________

I am proud to have a baby

______________________(brother - sister)

(Baby's name)_____________________is lucky to

have me for a big _________________________.

Was I ever that little?

You can discover the wonder of a brand-new baby:

Look at the baby's feet and toes.
Are they as big as yours?___Yes___No

Count the toes. How many are there?_____

Look at baby's footprint.
Does the baby have toenails?___Yes___No

How does baby's skin feel?
Is it smooth or rough?_______
What color is it?_________

Stroke the baby's skin gently.
Does the baby like to be touched?___Yes___No

Look at the baby's hands and fingers.
Have baby's fingernails been cut yet?
___Yes___No

When I put my finger inside baby's hand,
this happens:

____

When I touch one of baby's cheeks, this happens:

____

Very gently touch the baby's hair.
Is it soft? _____Yes____No

Ask your mom or dad why it is so important to be
careful of baby's head.

Look at the baby's lips:
Do baby's lips move even when he or she is not
eating? ____Yes____No
Can you see bumps where baby's teeth will
be?___Yes___No

Does the baby have eyelashes? ___Yes____No
Are they long or short?__________
Does baby open his or her eyes very often?___Yes___No

What sounds does baby make?

____
____
____

Does the baby cry_____softly or______ loudly?

Does the baby make a sound when eating?
What sound?______________________

When I gently touch one of baby's ears, this happens:____________________________

When baby hears a sudden sound, this happens:

____

When I gently touch the baby's lips, this happens:

____

____

What fun babies are!

What can baby do?

You may be surprised when you watch your new brother or sister and see how many things he or she can do already. Sit right next to the baby. Read each line on the chart on the next page and try to do it.

If **you can**, put an X under "I can." Then see if the baby can do the same thing. If you'd like help, your Mom or Dad can help you decide.

If **baby can**, put an X on the line. At the bottom of the chart, you can add some things you think of.

	I can	Baby can
• Hear noises	________	________
• See	________	________
• Taste	________	________
• Smell	________	________
• Feel	________	________
• Talk	________	________
• Cry	________	________
• Breathe	________	________
• Kick legs	________	________
• Wave arms	________	________
• Suck thumb	________	________
• Blink	________	________
• Understand	________	________
• Hum	________	________
• Sing	________	________
• Whistle	________	________
• Chew	________	________
• Swallow	________	________
• Walk	________	________
• Crawl	________	________
• Other things:		
	________	________
	________	________

MMMMMMMMM Baby talk OOOO

How does your baby brother or sister "talk" to you? When you need something, you can use words to tell your mom or dad, but what can the baby do?

I discover how baby talks to me!

"I am hungry" sounds like this:

....

"I am sleepy" sounds like this:

....

"I am too hot" sounds like this:

____

"I need to burp" sounds like this:

____

"I am uncomfortable" sounds like this:

....

"I am cold" sounds like this:

____

Can you guess what baby is telling you?

When you hear the baby crying, you get to play a game. You can try to guess what the baby is telling you. Your mom and dad played this game when you were a baby, too—so they will probably guess faster.

Here are some things I have learned:

1/ ______________________________

2/ ______________________________

3/ ______________________________

4/ ______________________________

5/ ______________________________

6/ ______________________________

7/ ______________________________

8/ ______________________________

I talk to baby

When?

Anytime the baby is awake and listening to you.

Where?

Sitting next to the baby.
Holding the baby.

Why?

So the baby can learn to talk
when he or she is bigger.
So the baby will learn to know your voice.
So the baby will feel loved.

What?

You can tell the baby about things that are happening around him or her. Like this:

"I just saw the puppy run by. Did you see the puppy run by? He was running fast!"

Write something you might say here:

....

....

____

....

You can tell the baby about something you are showing him or her, like this:

"Here is your blue rattle. It has yellow flowers on it and it makes a noise when I shake it."

Write something you might say here:

____

....

You can talk about the baby. Use the baby's name over and over like this:

"Look at Katy's long fingers! They are pretty fingers, Katy. I like to see Katy's pretty fingers."

Write something you might say here:

....

....

....

If you get tired of thinking of things to talk about, don't forget the baby loves to hear you **sing or hum a song!**

What will baby do all day?

Here is a place to record one day of baby's life. It will be fun to tell someone what the baby did all day!

Today, the baby had this many:

___diaper changes ___naps ___baths

___visitors ___changes of clothes

___"awake" times

Some more things baby did all day:

It won't be long until the baby
starts staying awake more and more
to watch what **you** are doing.

My
day

Here's how I spent one whole day:

How baby learns

How do you learn about the world? You see, hear, smell, touch, and taste to find out about things. You also can learn by asking other people about their favorite smells, sounds, tastes, and things to touch. You can guess about baby's, too.

♥

Person's name:______________________________

His or her favorite:

Smell____________________________________

Sound___________________________________

Taste____________________________________

Touch___________________________________

Person's name:______________________________

His or her favorite:

Smell______________________________

Sound______________________________

Taste______________________________

Touch______________________________

♥

My name:______________________________

My favorite:

Smell______________________________

Sound______________________________

Taste______________________________

Touch______________________________

I think
baby
would pick
these favorites:

♥ Smell________________________________

♥ Sound________________________________

♥ Taste________________________________

♥ Touch________________________________

♥

How we can play together

Playground rules:

Make sure either Mom or Dad tell you it's OK to play with baby!

Baby loves to see your face, so stay very close where he or she can see you.

If baby keeps watching you, he or she is having fun!

Baby loves to play the same game again and again!

If baby starts to cry, he or she may need to rest a moment.

Make certain baby still wants to play. He or she won't want to play if it is time to eat or sleep. Smile at the baby and give him or her a gentle hug or pat.

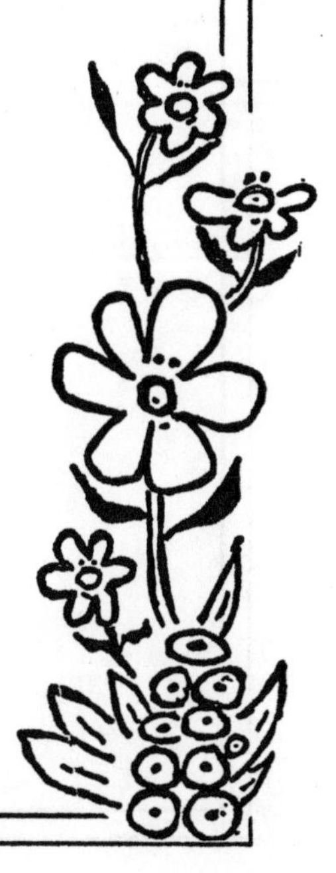

You can play when the baby's in a seat, swing, a
lap, on a bed or on a blanket on the floor.

Only play games that are safe for the baby.

Show the baby something bright and moving,
like a scarf, a pennant, a child's mobile,
or anything else your parents approve.
Keep it close to the baby so he or she can see it.
Let the baby touch what you are holding,
unless it could hurt the baby.

Show the baby a rattle and shake it.
Then move slowly around the room while you
shake the rattle and say the baby's name.

Sing a song and clap or do hand motions.
Move the baby's hands and feet while you sing.
Say a rhyme and do motions with your hands
and the baby's hands.

Play one of the baby games
you have learned.

BUZZ
BUZZ
BUZZ

What are they talking about?

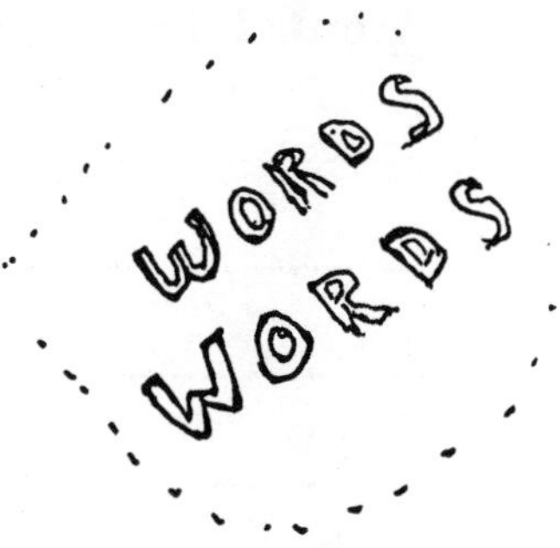

Have you heard words that you don't know? They are probably words about babies and baby things. You can write down the words here and ask an adult what they mean.

Words I don't know:	What the words mean:
....	....
....	....
....	....
________________	________________
....	....
....	....

MORE WORDS WORDS

Words I don't know:	What the words mean:

Have you heard these words?

Pediatrician
formula
gums

What they mean:

A **pediatrician** is a doctor just for babies and kids.
Formula is a special baby milk.
Gums are part of the mouth where baby's teeth grow (and so do yours).

My activity record with BABY

Here is a list of some fun things **baby and I** did:

Date	**What we did together:**
....	....
________________	________________________
....	....
....	....
....	....
________________	________________________
....	....
....	....

Dog-gone!

Here is a record of some ways I helped our family:

Date	I helped by:
....	....
....	....
....	....
....	....
....	....
....	....
....	....
....	....
....	....
....	....

Date	I helped by:

Date	I helped by:

The new baby is SPECIAL

Today my new baby________________is________days old.
(sister - brother) *(number)*

It seems like baby and I have had our pictures taken at least____________times.
(number)

So far, my favorite thing to do with baby is:

____

I like helping by:

____

____

I asked everyone
in the family to tell something
about the baby in only
ONE WORD.

Here is what they told me:

Mom:

____

Dad:

____

Others:

____

____

And here is what I think
is the **best word**
that tells about baby:

____

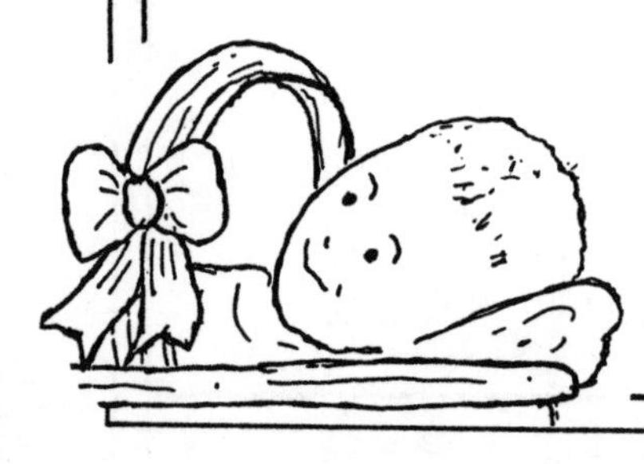

PART 5

WE GROW UP TOGETHER!

Your new baby brother or sister is growing and learning quickly. You will see how much fun you can have together.

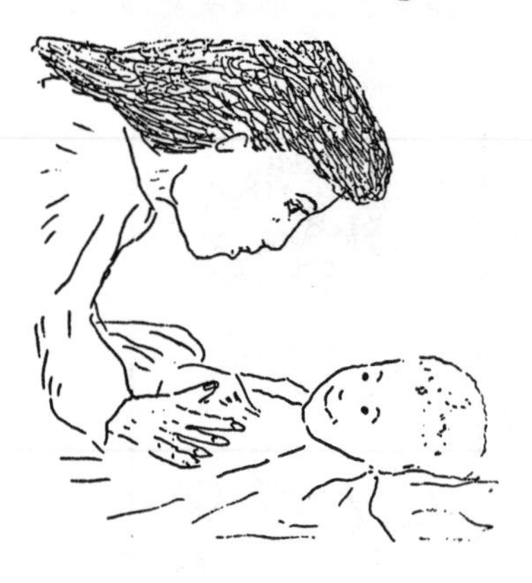

HOW CAN YOU TELL THE BABY IS LEARNING?

You may see that the baby stays awake more during the day. The baby may stop crying more quickly when he or she is picked up or fed. When you talk, the baby may make sounds back to you.

I am older, baby is younger

Have you been wondering how old you will be when your baby brother or sister has his or her first birthday? Here is a chart that will be fun to do and will show you your age and the baby's age for the next five years. On the first line, under *Me,* put your age right now. Finish the chart with your mom's or dad's help. When you read across each line, you can see the baby's age and your age at the same time.

Baby	Me
Newborn	________
1/2 year	________
1 year	________
1 1/2 years	________
2 years	________
2 1/2 years	________
3 years	________
3 1/2 years	________
4 years	________
4 1/2 years	________
5 years	________

Growing up special

As you and your new sister or brother get bigger and bigger, what do you think will be special about being kids together in the same family? Will it be special because you can plan surprises for mom and dad together? Or because you will have someone to play with, even on vacation? Here's a place to write what you think:

I think it will be special because:

....

....

....

....

....

....

Growing up friends!

Most moms and dads wish that their children always will be good friends. They may have ideas about how brothers and sisters get along. Ask your mom and dad what they wish for their kids as they grow up. You can write what they say here.

DAD

....

....

....

MOM

....

....

....

Other brothers and sisters

Ask one of your parents and a brother or a sister to remember something about their growing up together. Some might remember trips they made together, going to school, or sharing a room.

Name______________________________________

His or her favorite remembrance about growing up:

....

A favorite memory when they played together (playing a game, swimming, sledding):

....

What he or she said was the best thing about having a sister or a brother:

....

....

Name______________________________________

His or her favorite remembrance about growing up:

....

A favorite memory when they played together (playing a game, swimming, sledding):

....

What he or she said was the best thing about having a sister or a brother:

....

....

Name______________________________________

His or her favorite remembrance about growing up:

____

A favorite memory when they played together (playing a game, swimming, sledding):

____

What he or she said was the best thing about having a sister or a brother:

....

Baby's firsts!

You probably can't remember the first time you ate ice cream. But your parents can tell you about the surprised look on your face when you felt the cold and tasted the sweetness. You will have the fun of seeing your new baby brother or sister find out about the world. Be watching for Baby's Firsts and record them here. Have fun—but remember some may not happen right away.

Baby's first ice cream Date____________________

What happened: ....

....

....

Baby's first popsicle Date____________________

What happened: ....

....

Baby's first snow angel Date________________

What happened ....

....

Baby's first clapping Date____________________

What happened: ....

____

Baby's first somersault Date_______________

What happened: ....

....

Baby twirls around Date_______________________

What happened: ....

____

Baby's first trip down a slide Date_________

What happened: ....

....

Baby's first motorboat sound with mouth:

Date________________

What happened: ....

....

Baby sees soap bubbles: Date________________

What happened: ....

....

....

Baby's first trike ride: Date________________

What happened: ....

....

Baby's first time to say my name: Date___________

What happened: ....

....

....

....

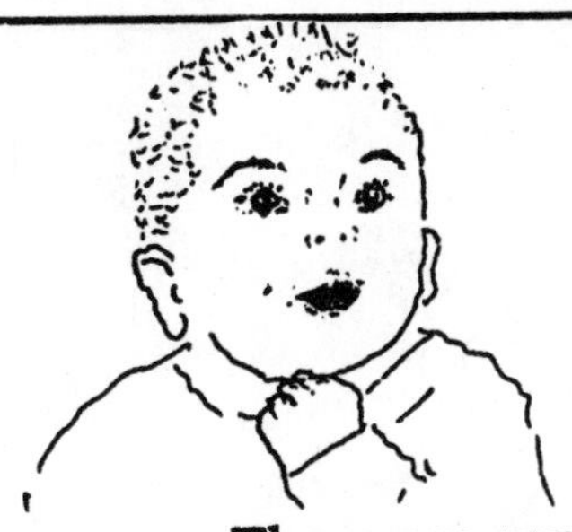

Baby's learning record

These are some of the important things baby has learned already:

Date ☆	Baby learned:

I love you

A special letter to baby

Dear_________________________:
(baby's name)

♥ It was a special day for all of us when you joined our family. I have been helping take care of you and I am excited that you will grow bigger and bigger so I can play with you more and more. When you are older, I will tell you all about when you were a baby and about the things we did together. But mostly I will tell you how much we have always loved you. Love,

My Name_____________________________________ ♥

Date____________________

♥